*To Mark and Carol
Best wishes to you both.
Philip Klinger*

FISHING ON THE SEA OF GALILEE

J. PHILIP KLINGER

THE COVER PHOTOGRAPH WAS TAKEN BY THE AUTHOR AT SUNRISE ON THE SEA OF GALILEE WITH THE GOLAN HEIGHTS IN THE BACKGROUND.

FISHING ON THE SEA OF GALIEE

FIRST EDITION
Copyright © 1995
J. Philip Klinger

All rights reserved. No portion of this book may be reproduced or utilized in any form or by any means, electronic or mechanical including photocopying, without permission in writing from the publisher. Inquiries should be addressed to: J. Philip Klinger, 119 E. Center Street, Warsaw, IN 46580.

Library of Congress Catalog Card Number: 94-96813

ISBN 1-55673-981-8 PRINTED IN U.S.A.

DEDICATION

For Nancy, an incarnational teacher, and the congregations
I have served who inspired me to be an incarnational preacher.

>I am a part of all that I have met.
>Yet all experience is an arch where-thro'
>Gleams that untravell'd world, whose margin fades
>Forever and forever when I move.
>
>>ULYSSES
>>Alfred, Lord Tennyson

TABLE OF CONTENTS

	PAGE
CHAPTER ONE FISHING ON THE SEA OF GALILEE	11
CHAPTER TWO WHAT HAVE YOU DONE WITH MY JESUS?	17
CHAPTER THREE FINCH FEEDERS, ARROWHEADS AND HOSPITALITY	23
CHAPTER FOUR THE GOSPEL ACCORDING TO *HOOSIERS*	29
CHAPTER FIVE I PLANTED A GARDEN	35
CHAPTER SIX GARAGE SALE THEOLOGY AND OTHER MOVING EXPERIENCES	41
CHAPTER SEVEN A LETTER FROM HOME	47
CHAPTER EIGHT WORSHIP AND THE THEATRE	53
CHAPTER NINE WHAT KEEPS US LISTENING	59
CHAPTER TEN LEADERSHIP AND *THE LION KING*	67

FOREWORD

I like sermons that connect with life that touch the human spirit and condition. This collection of sermons, by Dr. J. Philip Klinger, does just that - they not only reflect life - they transcend it. The author not only tells it like it is, but how it should be!

Sermons are actually the preached Word, they are to be heard. Klinger has the ability to take words created to be heard and fashion them in such a manner that they read well. His illustrations will touch the reader and always seem appropriate, well placed and timed.

This book will not only give the reader insight into life and faith, but will illustrate the faith of the Preacher. Preachers should never be mere objective observers, reporting on what they see. Reading these sermons will provide glimpses into the faith - struggles, questions and joys of the Preacher.

It is not always easy to permit ancient texts to retain their historical integrity while giving them fresh, contemporary application and relevance. These sermons have a freshness, a relevance that will speak to new and young searchers for truth. The seasoned Faith Traveler will be nourished as well, as the old and familiar story is linked to today's pains and hope.

What I found most refreshing in these sermons is that they are truly Good News! So many preachers specialize, even delight in reporting Bad News! Every sermon here has a note of hope, promise, grace.

I believe what is needed in these times of turmoil, inexplicable suffering and violence, complex changing ethical and moral standards, is a kind of compass to assist us in moving through such a confusing maze. These sermons are just such a guide.

As you read these powerful messages you will be made to think and feel. You will be challenged. There will be times when you will smile or want to cry. But you will be moved and hopefully changed. So I commend these sermons to the reader and echo the words of Klinger when he writes,

"I invite you to start fishing in deep waters. It may be a deeper, more significant life. It may be a faith which needs to be rebuilt. Or it may be that you are struggling with God's **call** for your life. May God give you strength as you answer the call to deep waters."

Woodie W. White, Bishop
Indiana Area
The United Methodist Church

INTRODUCTION

Preaching is incarnational. The old definition of Phillips Brooks that preaching is "truth through personality" is still a good definition today. This volume of sermons is intended to demonstrate that preaching can be both incarnational and exegetically responsible.

These sermons were preached at First United Methodist Church at Purdue University. They encompass eleven years in that great pulpit. I am profoundly grateful to the congregation of First Church for the privilege of preaching to faculty, students, staff, as well as townspeople and business leaders.

The opening sermon from which the book takes its title was based on a first-time visit to the Holy Land. The experience of actually fishing on the Sea of Galilee was instrumental in my move to a more informal style of preaching as narrative, or story-telling.

"What Have You Done With My Jesus?" was first delivered to the North Central Jurisdictional Course of Study at Garrett-Evangelical Theological Seminary at Northwestern University. It traces the shift in theological education in the last thirty years. It is a kind of parable of what is happening in the Church today.

Two of the sermons in this collection are based on recent movies. "The Gospel According to *Hoosiers*" is both a personal account of my own experience growing up as a basketball player in Indiana and a response to the movie version of an actual event in Indiana basketball history. The meditation "Leadership and *The Lion King*" was first delivered to the North Indiana Cabinet and later to the ministers of the Warsaw District of The United Methodist Church. What purports to be a simple child's tale has insights that any potential leader, ecclesiastical or secular, needs to consider.

The sermon "Finch Feeders, Arrowheads, and Hospitality" is a sermon on evangelism, or as the popular phrase has it today, Church Growth. The implication is that outreach must be intentional and anyone can participate.

I have included a farewell sermon, "I Planted a Garden," to demonstrate the use of narrative and allegory in a highly emotionally charged event. Leaving a beloved congregation is always difficult. The need to pave the way for one's successor is critical.

The sermon "Garage Sale Theology and Other Moving Experiences" captures a growing phenomenon in urban culture and is a commentary on our disposable society. Jesus used common everyday experiences in his preaching. There are lessons to be learned in any encounter. The study of "living human documents" can be a powerful learning tool.

The sermon "A Letter From Home" was delivered on the first Sunday that students returned to the University. It encompasses all of our fears and hopes as students leave home and parents let them go.

I have included a teaching sermon, "Worship and The Theatre" as an example of the need for preaching to be didactic. The sermon was preached in response to an ongoing debate over what worship should be like in the life of the Church. The debate is still raging over whether worship should be subjective or objective. It is, or course, both.

The final selection is a dialogue sermon written with Jim Pender. "What Keeps Us Listening" is different in style, format, and content. It encompasses the dramatic element which is often needed to get across the message of John 1.

I want to express my appreciation to the staff of First United Methodist Church in West Lafayette, Indiana, and especially Irma Stevens, Sharon Dull, Deb Downey, and Bryan Ton who helped prepare this manuscript.

Special appreciation is given to Bishop Woodie W. White of the Indiana Area of The United Methodist Church for his generous foreward and to Lyle Schaller for his encouragement. I want to thank my wife Nancy, a steadfast partner in ministry who is also an "incarnational teacher," and our sons, Geoffrey and Kevin, for their inspiration and support.

CHAPTER ONE

FISHING ON THE SEA OF GALILEE

Luke 5:1-11

I have been waiting for two years for this text to come up in the lectionary. The reason should be obvious by now. It recalls for me the most powerful personal experience of my ministry. You see, "Fishing on the Sea of Galilee" is not just the title of a sermon. It is something I did.

For those of you who are new, I was invited to join a Holy Land Pilgrimage in February of 1990. It was offered to me by the Knights Templar organization and I was nominated by members of this congregation to participate with seventy-eight ministers from several different denominations. It was a high-water mark of my ministry. I had traveled around the world but had never seen the places I had been preaching about for thirty years.

The trip fulfilled all my hopes and dreams. The usual stops were observed, Jerusalem, Cana, Jericho, the Dead Sea. But the greatest thrill came late at night on the Sea of Galilee itself. We were staying at the kibbutz, Nof Ginnosar. A kibbutz is a self-contained community where every one contributes his or her abilities for the good of the whole. I learned upon arrival that the kibbutz had a fishing program. Late that evening I went to the front desk to inquire if I could join them that evening. The clerk said no one had ever done that before. I quickly added that I would be willing to work. As the clerk called the captain I said a little prayer for I had dreamed of this moment since I was a child fishing in the Wildcat Creek and reading about Jesus and the call of the fishermen to be his disciples.

In a few moments the clerk returned and said one of the crew was sick and they would have a place for me. I knew right then it was going to be a great night. I asked the clerk where to find the crew and he said there was a jetty about a mile down the beach. I would meet them at 11:00 p.m. I went to my room and swore my roommate to secrecy, borrowed his rain-gear and set out for the greatest adventure of my life.

When I arrived at the "beach" I discovered it was not like the white sands of Florida, but mud and reeds in both directions. I also realized I forgot to ask which direction along the beach. So I looked left and right and decided to go left. I soon discovered that I was walking ankle-deep in mud and pushing my way through reeds taller than my head. At that moment it occurred to me that except for the captain no one knew I was coming and the reality of where I was hit me full force. What if someone thought I was a terrorist infiltrating the kibbutz? After all, Syria was just on the other side of the lake. After a few moments of stark fear, I pushed on and soon I saw the outline of a rock formation and decided that must be the jetty. Imagine my relief when I saw the dock and found the fishing boat tied up next to it. I was a few minutes early, so I took the opportunity to clean off my sneakers and try to look half-way presentable. In a few minutes the captain ambled down to the dock followed by three other very sleepy fishermen. They looked at me with a certain disdain and began their preparations to begin a night's work. Fortunately, the captain, whose name was David, spoke English as did one other fisherman. He informed them of my mission and then asked if I wanted to work or just ride along. Well, no self-respecting fisherman could turn down that offer. He showed me my post which was tending the nets. I was to keep the nets straight before and after each catch. It wasn't as easy as it looked. It was hard work. David suggested after my first effort, "You'll do better next time." I knew by that comment that I had messed up.

We began like every other fishing trip I have ever been on, riding for an hour to the other end of the lake. Why is it that the fish are always at the opposite shore from where the boat is? It seems to be one of the certainties of fishing. When we arrived we discovered that the light boats had been tampered with, either by the PLO or local fishermen who resented the commercial operation. So we relit the lamps and began circling with the nets. The first few passes were not very productive. I had a sinking feeling that I had been here before. Like the time I sailed around Puget

Sound looking for salmon and came home empty-handed. I think I paid one hundred dollars for the privilege.

So I walked up to the front of the boat and I prayed a prayer something like this, "Lord, you showed the disciples what to do, give me some sign. I am one of your disciples. Give me a small miracle. I remembered the story from our text and went up to the captain, "David, why don't we go out into deeper water and try our luck there?" How's that for originality? He looked at me with a quizzical expression and said, "O.K."

Once again, we put out the light boats, circled the net with the trawler and waited for the nets to sink to the bottom. Imagine my joy, when the winch began to groan and the net came up bulging with Sardines (which is what we were fishing for), catfish, eels, and St. Peter's fish (a local delicacy and the fish in whose mouth Jesus found a coin). It went like this for the rest of the night. By seven in the morning we had caught seven and one-half tons of sardines, or about three thousand dollars for the kibbutz.

Throughout the night we would take small breaks to eat oranges and drink coffee in the cabin below the deck. The youngest member of the crew, Uwe, asked me if I knew that Jesus didn't die on the cross, but went to India to establish a branch of Mysticism. I tried, without offending him to present the resurrection faith. He was thirty-five, not married and a bit of a secular humanist. Another fisherman was an engineer with two patents for medical breakthroughs on pain, who gave it up to become a fisherman.

By morning light our trawler was towing four cargo boats loaded to the brim with sardines. As the sun rose over the Golan Heights I realized that I had been a part of a magical, mystical moment. What was a mundane night of work for these four Jewish fishermen was for me a poignant moment with God. How like life that is!

> Earth's crammed with heaven,
> And every common bush afire with God;
> But only he who sees, takes off his shoes,
> The rest sit round it and pluck blackberries.
> Aurora Leigh

What Elizabeth Barrett Browning is suggesting to us is that the ordinariness of life can be a sacrament for some and for others a drudgery.

I think this is why Jesus chose common elements to convey the deepest truths about himself and about God. The common everyday ingredients of bread and wine become a mystery in the hands of God.

When I came home from fishing on the Sea of Galilee I didn't tell any of my colleagues or the guides about my experience. First of all, I wanted to savor the experience; and secondly, I knew what their reaction would be. Sure enough, when on our last night we were asked to share our "highlight," the reactions were all the same: "Why didn't you take me with you?"

I tell you this story today because I believe what happened to Peter and James and John can happen to you. It happened to me because I was looking for an Epiphany. You don't have to get into a boat in the middle of night with a group of strange Jewish fishermen to meet God. But if you are looking for God in your everyday life you can find God. In a friend, in the woods, in a flower, in a poem, maybe even in Church. It helps if you are looking. It helps more if you pray to find God. But don't ever believe that what happened to the disciples and to me can't happen to you. If you do you will be missing one of the greatest adventures in life.

I haven't always been attracted to deep water. One day when I was a very little boy, two of my friends and I decided to take a trip to the swimming hole in Wildcat Creek. Things were going well until one of the boys yelled, "Hey, Phil, come on out here into the deep water." Suddenly my heart panicked with fear, and I could feel my pulse quicken. For you see, I was afraid of deep water. So I pretended I didn't hear my friend and went splashing around the edges of the water, making noises and chasing frogs. Eventually I was able to overcome this fear of deep water, but it took practice, confidence and faith in myself. So you see, from the beginning, deep water has been a challenge for me.

Jesus commanded his disciples to cast their nets on the other side, and when they did so, they came up with a great catch of fish. The simple meaning of this story is that Simon, James and

John were fishing in the wrong place. They had cast their nets in shallow waters. There is a challenge in this story which confronts us at the very base of our existence. The deeper truth of this story is that shallow water is synonymous with shallow living. All too often like Simon, the fisherman, we discover ourselves fishing in the wrong places. Our system of values is out of focus.

Everyone values some things and fails to value others. The things one values line up in a priority scale. A man may value both money and his wife, but he may value the first more than the second. When there is a conflict between an opportunity to acquire the first and nurture love for the second, this man will choose in only one way. So, too, a man may be loyal to his church and loyal to his club, but when his club holds an outing on Sunday morning, he may place the latter above the former as a claim upon him.

Jesus told the fishermen to put out into the deep. They responded, and they got the results that they would not have won if they had stayed in the shallows by the shore. Whether it was meant so or not, this has become a symbol of what would happen for their souls. When Peter and the others were called to leave their fishing boats and to follow Jesus on an unpredictable way and into what would prove to be a costly allegiance, they were putting out into deep waters. Paul was putting out into the deep when he launched the mission to the Gentiles. All the great pioneers and evangelists have done the same.

When you launch out into the deep there are new invitations, new challenges and new surprises.

There are new invitations in the imperative command, "cast out." Those who have been fishing in the shallow waters of life will be challenged to reach deeper levels of living.

There are new challenges in the implied directive: "try another way." Have you ever tried everything and nothing worked, except for that one additional 'try,' right after you had quit trying. The challenge is to never give up. If we had stopped after the first few tries with the light boats on the Sea of Galilee, we would have come home empty-handed. Don't stop too soon in trying to overcome the obstacles in your life.

There are new surprises like a net filled with fish and a life filled with love. God's grace is always going ahead of us and delighting us with unexpected results.

I invite you to start fishing in deeper waters. It may be a deeper, more significant life. It may be a faith which needs to be rebuilt. Or it may be that you are struggling with God's call for your life. May God give you strength as you answer the call to deep water.

CHAPTER TWO

WHAT HAVE YOU DONE WITH MY JESUS?

John 20:1-18

In 1961 a young seminarian walked through the massive oak doors that served as the entrance to the Gothic foyer of what was then known as Garrett Biblical Institute. I was that student. Greeting the visitors in front of the library entrance was a plaster reproduction of a statue of Christ by the Danish sculptor, Thorvaldsen. First commissioned in Copenhagen in 1821, the original still resides in the Church of Our Lady.

It was commonly assumed that a statue of Christ was a fitting symbol for a Biblical Institute. However, there were students, fresh from the fifties, who thought it was amusing to adorn the statue with a football helmet, a scarf around the neck, and one time a cigar was found between Christ's fingers. An occasional pious student asked the question, "What have you done with my Jesus?"

In 1972 I returned to what was then called Garrett Theological Seminary as the Director of Admissions. I looked for the statue of Christ, but it was gone. It had been moved to the entrance of the Chapel. Its broken fingers had been restored from the vandalism of the Day of Rage when the SDS and the Weathermen had occupied the Seminary. There are stories floating around about Trustee meetings when the statue was dressed up and put in the meeting room. Fingers were broken again. Signs were painted on the statue. Announcements were taped on the torso to inform students of caucus meetings and counter-cultural events. Alumni and friends frequently came back to the Seminary and asked, "What have you done with my Jesus?"

Administrators, hard-pressed to deal with an icon which had become an object of ridicule and a joke, moved the statue to the end of the hall on the third floor, where it began to gather dust along with the other reproductions of biblical archaeology. It stayed there for several years, until years later it was placed in the attic for storage. Occasionally staff and faculty, who had remembered earlier days, asked the rhetorical question to themselves, "What have you done with my Jesus?"

When I asked this year about the statue, it was reported that one day when the attic was being cleaned out, the statue of Christ, whose movements throughout the Seminary I have chronicled, was no longer there!

On Easter morning, Mary Magdalene came to the garden tomb in the darkness. She was the first one there. When she found the stone rolled away, she went to Simon Peter and the one whom Jesus loved (we assume that was John) and told them that someone had taken him from the tomb, and she did not know where they had laid him (John 20:2). Peter and John left to go back to tell the disciples, but Mary stayed at the tomb. Again, she looked into the tomb and saw two angels who asked her why she was weeping. Once more, she replied, "They have taken away my Lord, and I do not know where they have taken him." (John 20:12).

Here is Mary, going to stare into the darkness of the tomb, weeping for what might have been. Here is Mary, in a shaded world, a shadow meeting another shadow, whom she supposed to be the gardener, a tender of deathbeds.

But he isn't the gardener. He is one who comes out of the darkest of darknesses and knows her name and speaks it, "Mary." This is not merely a voice or a spirit or a word mysteriously scrawled on a rock. This is a person, a living person, reaching out and speaking to another person, saying "Mary."

Standing in the very eye of that upheavaled and violently still, hurricaned morning, Mary has the faith and the courage and the presence of grace to answer, "Rabboni!" Here is all the love and life she had sent hopelessly into the depths now returned--to her, personally. Here is nothing less than the complete victory and vindication of love in Jesus' naming of the woman and her response.

He, Jesus, had been dead. There was no doubt about **that**. A hundred pounds of spices had been stuffed into the black tomb with his dead body, and now that tomb, unplugged and open to the air, was redolent of the sickening-sweet, too-obviously disguised smell of death. He, Jesus, had been carried dead into the black, hungry maw that is the destiny of all people. Every hammer blow on the cross had been the sound of another door closing; and then the last door was rolled into place, and Jesus' time was closed and his life was canceled out.

Jesus came to an end behind that last door. There is no mistaking that. But the door opened again--I do not know how, God knows. But the door did open; the same door that death had shut, God opened. And so God made the end into a new beginning.

It was not until Mary encountered the risen Christ, supposing him to be the gardener, that she discovered the amazing surprise of the resurrection. Hoping to care for the physical body, she discovered that Christ was ahead of her. The Christ of Easter surprise, who was born in a stable manger, died on an instrument of shame, was buried in a borrowed tomb, had one more surprise for his followers. He always goes ahead of us, his disciples, and especially his Church.

We look to the Seminary for guidance and inspiration. He is not here! The "Case of the Missing Jesus" should serve as a reminder of what has happened in this Seminary and by extension in the Church in the last thirty years. We have embraced every cause but Christ in a feeble attempt to relate the gospel to the present culture. We put our spiritual and theological fingers in the air in a desperate attempt to sense which way the wind is blowing and set our sails in that direction, and Christ goes on ahead of us.

We have tried to be amateur sociologists discussing little trends in religion. We have tried to imitate the psychologists discussing our personality adjustments. We try to discuss the scientific agenda with our new philosophy and forget that "Athens has nothing to do with Jerusalem." It's true that philosophy has been the handmaiden of theology, but how many people have ever been argued into the Kingdom of God? Not many! We try to do everything but what we were called to do, "Preach Christ, and him crucified." Our membership has declined for one simple reason over the last thirty years. We have failed to take Wesley's advice to

Coke, Whatley and Vesey as they sailed from Bristol to America to "Offer them Christ." We have replaced the traditional view of evangelism with a new doctrine of pluralism. We have elevated pluralism to a theological category. To paraphrase a spokesman of another generation, pluralism as a theological category is no virtue, pluralism as a sociological description is no vice. United Methodism, "What have you done with my Jesus?"

Maybe one of the surprises Christ has for us is that he is more interested in Christianity than in Churchianity. Perhaps we will discover that the work of the kingdom is more pleasing to Christ than spinning the wheels of the denomination. Whenever we try to put a box around Christ, he breaks out of the mold and goes on ahead of us. That includes plaster statutes and fixed theologies. The only Christ that matters is the relational Christ who comes to us in the midst of resurrection faith. Mary knew him when he spoke her name. He called her, "Mary." She turned and said to him in Hebrew, "Rabboni" (which means Teacher (John 20:16)). Here is the early Church offering a theology of relationship.

Friends, what is your relationship with Christ this Easter morning? As you walk in the garden of doubt, discouragement, and despair, will you know who is speaking when you return to the voice of the One who first called you? Friends, "What have you done with your Jesus?"

A little over a year ago, Nancy and I attended the Donors' Dinner at Wesley Manor, a retirement home of North Indiana Conference. After the meeting, a beautiful woman in her mid eighties came up to me and said, "I heard your name. Are you any relation to Don Klinger?" I said, "He was my father." She said, "I used to date your father, before he met your mother. He used to come over to my dorm and play the saxophone for me." I said, "I still have that saxophone, even though it hasn't been out of the case for more than forty years." My father played in a Jazz Band that toured the country in the Twenties before he went into the ministry.

That night an idea formed in my head. I would take that old saxophone and have it restored. It is an old C Melody instrument which is now in perfect condition, shiny silver and gold, and even though they don't make them any more, it still is capable of beautiful music. I have been taking lessons for the past three months. This year before the Donor's Dinner, we stopped at her home. I played "Love's Old Sweet Song" and "My Wild Irish Rose" as the tears rolled down both our cheeks.

There are some things death cannot take away. A memory is one of them. If the song is to continue, we must do the singing.

The truth of the Easter faith is relational. When all the books have been read, all the exams passed, all the sermons preached, all the calls made, there will only be one question that really matters: "What have you done with my Jesus?"

CHAPTER THREE
FINCH FEEDERS, ARROWHEADS AND HOSPITALITY

Romans 5:19

I grew up in a little place between Greentown and Kokomo, Indiana. We lived in several different places, but most of my childhood was spent on Sycamore Road near the Wildcat Creek just about a mile from the Vermont Elevator. We used to ride our bikes over to the Vermont Elevator to get a Coke. That's when Cokes were a nickel and you looked at the bottom to see who got the free Coke because the one whose bottle was manufactured farthest away always got the free Coca Cola at the Vermont Elevator. Vermont consisted of an elevator and two houses. We used to drag race with the Amish horse and buggies until they learned how to run us off the road on our bicycles then we stopped doing that.

We had a party line on our telephone. How many of you remember party lines? We had 17 on our party line including the parsonage and calling the minister was like telling everybody your troubles, so people came to our father's house rather than call on the telephone.

Charlie Kurtz was a farmer in the community and Charlie was always trying to use the phone. Between 2 and 4 in the afternoon, there were two people who always had the phone tied up telling the news. He would pick up and they would say, "Somebody's picking up the telephone." He would put it back down. Finally one day he got tired of it and he picked up the phone and said, "Excuse me ladies, but I have to report a death." "Oh, certainly, well of course." And they clicked, clicked and hung up the phone. He got Central and then called the glue factory to come and pick up one of his dead cows. They had picked back up to find out who had died and they never forgave Charlie Kurtz for that little trick.

My father died when I was 13. After his death, my family stayed in the community. His memory has always been very important to me and my ministry. Recently, when I went to Wabash to put flowers on my father's grave, I noticed something I hadn't seen in 40 years. I have a ring that has a cross on it. It's a birthstone for the month of August and I put a simple Latin cross on it. I noticed on my father's gravestone there is a simple Latin cross in exactly the same proportion on his gravestone. I never really remember seeing that, but I suppose something in my subconscious made me want to do that with my ring.

Those influences of our past, our growing-up years never do leave us. For good or for ill. We honor our fathers today on this Father's Day. I want to tell you a story about another father, a friend of mine. As we begin I'd like to recall the words of Romans 5 that were read a few moments ago, the 19th verse: "So by one man's obedience many will be made righteous."

Let's pray about that. Lord, may the words of my mouth and the meditations of our hearts be acceptable in thy sight, O Lord, our strength and our Redeemer. Amen.

The story I want to tell you is about a man named Carl Rose. He's a very important person in my life. He was a newspaper man who became a poultry man and opened a hatchery in a feed store in South Bend. The store was in a rather seedy part of town and yet it was very successful. Carl went on a mission trip with me to Haiti to help the Haitians improve their poultry production. He taught me a great deal about stewardship. He sold me on the idea of the congregational dinner which we have implemented here with great success. We come together for a dinner and simply tell our story. We don't take pledges. The Church helps to pay for the dinner to enable everyone to come. I don't want to talk about stewardship or about Haiti or about poultry. I want to talk with you a little bit about Carl as a businessman.

One day as I was going into his store after the customers had left, I noticed some tubes that were hanging behind the counter. I said, "What are those, Carl?" He said, "Why, that's a finch feeder." I said, "A what?" He said, "A finch feeder. You put thistle seed into it and hang it outdoors and the finches will come and feed." I said, "Carl, I've been living here six years now and I have never yet seen a goldfinch in this community." With a twinkle in his eye and a smile on his face, he said, "I'll tell you what, I'll give you one of these finch feeders. I'll even give you the seed to put into it and I guarantee you that within 24 hours you will have goldfinches hanging on that feeder." I said, "You're on." So I took it home and I put the thistle seed in it and I hung it out on the tree in the backyard and watched from the kitchen. It wasn't in 24 hours, but in 6 hours. That evening there were eight goldfinches, with beautiful yellow and black feathers perched on that feeder. They were feeding furiously. You could almost literally watch the thistle seed go down.

What Carl Rose knew as a businessman was that I would be coming back to buy more thistle seed very soon. And of course, I did. If you know the price of thistle seed, you know he wasn't such a bad businessman after all. He didn't really **give** me the feeder.

Now, I really don't want to talk about business. I want to talk to you about the symbol of that finch feeder for the Church. That finch feeder is the Church. The seed is the word of God, and the programs we offer here at First Church. Those finches that were out there in the bushes, in the trees, and beyond are the people of this community who have not yet found a Church. Like those goldfinches, I believe there are people out there, waiting to be fed. If we feed them, they will come!

I received a brochure in the mail the other day from our Conference office. It plotted the counties of the State of Indiana. Someone had done a demographic survey and told what percentage of people in each county were unchurched. With all the Churches in this community can you believe that over 50% of the people in Tippecanoe County are unchurched? Dear friends, they are out there. They are waiting for an invitation from someone like you and me. You have over 10 people in your life who are in your sphere of influence who are friends, neighbors, family members who may not be in a church. When was the last time you invited them or brought them to church with you? They're out there. They're waiting to be fed. And if we will just offer them the opportunity and let it be known that there is food available at First United Methodist Church in West Lafayette, they'll come. I never put the feed out in the finch feeder in our backyard without thinking of Carl Rose and how "one man's obedience has led many to righteousness."

Thinking back again to those childhood days near the Wildcat Creek, I remember the church that my father served. It's a brick church, but I always used to think of it as the Little Brown Church in the Vale. If we had more time we'd sing "The Church in the Wildwood" this morning. It is one of my favorite songs from my youth.

The Wildcat Creek sort of wound around until they filled it up and made a reservoir for the town of Kokomo. Now the church overlooks the big reservoir. The Vermont Elevator is still only about a mile away. The Miami Indians once lived in that area. As a boy, once in a while I would stumble across an arrowhead like this one. This is the first arrowhead I ever found. I found it just this side of the Wildcat Creek at the edge of a plowed field. I know there are treasures for anyone who can find them.

I was reminded of that experience at Annual Conference when someone told the story about two farmers who lived next door to each other on 140 acre farms. One farmer went into the other farmer's house one day and noticed in the kitchen shelf after shelf of arrowheads. He said, "I don't understand it. We have adjoining farms and I have never found an arrowhead, and yet here you are with all of these arrowheads. Where did you get them?" He said, "I found them plowing outside, in the field, along the drive, by the woods edge." The other farmer said, "But I've never found any arrowheads. What's your secret?" "Oh, it's quite simple," he said. "When I get up in the morning I *think arrowheads*. When I go out to feed the cows I *think arrowheads*. When I get on the tractor and begin to plow, I am always *thinking arrowheads*. When I'm finished for the day and I go out for a walk along the woods, I *think arrowheads*. That's why I have all of these arrowheads and you have none."

I thought about that in relationship to our Church and the finch feeders and evangelism. When will we begin to *think arrowheads* like church growth and inviting people to church?

When does the church come up in our conversation quite naturally with people we work with, or with our next door neighbors over the back fence? Do we mention the Church to family members who are not participating or involved? When we begin to *think arrowheads* then maybe our Church will begin to grow at the level and rate that God wants it to. It won't happen unless everyone who is in this congregation takes responsibility and reaches out the hand of friendship. They're out there in the bushes, beyond the trees, beyond our eye's horizon. Waiting. Waiting for your invitation and mine.

Our Work Area on Evangelism this fall will be sending out some brochures inviting people to come to First Church. That won't be enough unless they come and are received and are fed. That is the third point I'd like to make this morning. That is, when people come, do we offer the hand of hospitality? Do we create space for strangers in our congregation and in our lives as Abraham did at Mamre when the three strangers welcomed him and they turned out to be angels of the Lord? Or as the widow of Zerafaf did for Ezekiel, and then after she had invited him in she discovered who he was - a man of God. This was the miracle of the dead son who was raised. We recall the sad journey of the two who walked along the road to Emmaus. Not knowing who this stranger was, they entered into conversation with him until, through their hospitality, they allowed Him to show them who He was by an act of hospitality.

Henry Nouwen, the great Dutch theologian, wrote a book a few years ago called, *Reaching Out*. He suggests there are three movements in the spiritual life. The second movement is from hostility to hospitality. The Dutch have a word for guesthouse that takes in the meaning of the word hospitality. Do we make our church a place of hospitality?

Susan Ruach, Council Director for the South Indiana Conference, visits a lot of churches. In one church she went down to their coffee hour and saw a young woman come into the church wearing blue jeans and a jean jacket. Two members went immediately to that woman, and engaged her in conversation. Two other people came in and started to wander through the coffee hour. It soon became apparent they were going to walk out. She said, "The spirit of friendship in that group was so contagious I went over as a stranger and welcomed these two new people to that congregation." She was impressed. She said, "unfortunately there are some churches she has visited where that's not the case."

That happened to me one time on vacation in Fort Lauderdale, Florida. I decided to try a United Methodist Church and I stood deliberately thirty-five minutes in a coffee hour without a single person ever speaking to me. I know the feeling of isolation and loneliness of being a stranger and not receiving a welcome. I pray that it never happens here. I pray that we will be intentional about our hospitality. I pray that we will create a space for strangers to be welcomed in. We have a unique ministry for students in this community. Last evening we were in the home of one of our members whose fellowship room was cluttered with furniture. I asked if they had opened a furniture store. They said no, they were storing furniture for an undergraduate student who had been working in our church and is gone for the summer. I thought, what a tremendous act of hospitality.

We all have that opportunity to reach out to the students who are in our midst who may go on from here. We do it not because they will someday join our church, but because that is the hospitable thing to do. Sometimes you cast your bread on the waters and it does come back to you. In the little town of Economy, Indiana there was a man who had made his fortune. He sent several hundred thousand dollars to this little church because as a little boy in a poor family that church had provided shoes for him and his brothers and sisters and he never forgot that act of hospitality.

What I'm saying this morning is that the people are out there. The finch feeder is an example of the fact that people are waiting to be fed. But we've got to *think arrowheads*. We've got to think church growth. We've got to think inviting people personally and directly. When they come, we've got to offer a space of welcoming not only into the Church, but into our lives. I suppose I could close by saying, "Well, that's the news from First Church, where all the people are hospitable, and all the people care, and all the people are setting good examples. "So by one person's righteousness many will be made righteous." I pray to God it will be so."

CHAPTER FOUR
THE GOSPEL ACCORDING TO "HOOSIERS"

II Timothy 2:1-7; 4:6-8
Matthew 3:23-27

The year was 1952. A broken down coach drives his Chevrolet through the central Indiana countryside. He has just been named basketball coach and history teacher of Hickory High School, population 68. A man with an unsavory past, he is trying one more time to catch the "brass ring" so commonly sought by coaches and players alike.

He finds himself criticized by the townspeople before he begins. He is undermined by a fellow teacher, he is sabotaged by the very players he is trying to coach. There is a school referendum and he is voted out of his job until the star player comes out of retirement, to announce that he will play only if Coach Dale stays. He does, and of course, their winning ways begin, leading ultimately to the State Championship. In the process he wins the girl, wins the fans, and wins his self-respect.

It is, of course, the retelling of the story of the Milan basketball story of 1954 when Coach Marvin Wood with Bobby Plump and Ray Craft won the championship from highly ranked, and powerful Muncie Central.

It is also **our** story, for every one who ever went to a small high school or attended an Indiana basketball game can find something familiar. It is also **my** story, for before I was a preacher I was a basketball player. I learned to play basketball in the Howard Township gym where Bob Troyer went to school. The end of the gym was even with the basket so you had to put out your foot to keep from hitting the wall. The ceiling was so low you learned to shoot line drives, instead of arching your shots. I remember a group of farmers getting up a petition in 1953 to get rid of my coach, it was eventually reversed by the Trustees, and the next year our consolidated school beat Kokomo when they were ranked Number

One in the state. But more importantly, it is the **Gospel** story. I see in the much celebrated and highly recommended movie "*Hoosiers*" three truths that reflect Christian values we can live with and by.

I. FIRST, THE GOSPEL ACCORDING TO "HOOSIERS" ILLUSTRATES THE NEED FOR DISCIPLINE.

When Coach Dale arrived in little Hickory, he inherited a group of "shooters" who knew very little about fundamentals and team spirit. They were all individuals who knew how to take care of themselves but were not willing to "pay the price," to pommel their bodies and subdue them, as St. Paul suggests in order to achieve their very best. In short, they were undisciplined.

In one memorable scene Coach Dale gathered the players for their first session and found that two players were carrying on their own conversation, totally ignoring what he was trying to say. He stopped in mid-sentence and asked if what they were discussing was more important than what he was telling them, and then suggested they leave the practice floor and not come back until they were willing to give their total attention.

He then set up some wooden chairs and had them begin to work on dribbling and passing the basketball and running wind sprints until they were in shape and had mastered the fundamentals of the game. No scrimmage. No horsing around. Just the basics.

As I thought about the spiritual life, I concluded that we would be a lot better off if we would practice the presence of God, read our Bibles and pray more often, we wouldn't be such strangers to our faith. We expect to "win the championship" of faith but are not willing to pay the price in order to make it happen. We all need more spiritual discipline. We are spiritually lazy.

In the Church we need to practice discipline. Once in a while an individual or group of individuals feel they can go their own way. Things aren't going like they want so they pull away and snipe, and sabotage, and undermine existing programs and the result is dissension, mistrust, and a divided congregation. Coach Dale had to break the party spirit, "The we've never done it that way before" spirit, in order to show them what a team spirit was. No one individual was more important than any other individual. They began to win when they became a team. He or she who has ears to hear, let them hear the message of the "Gospel According to Hoosiers" concerning our need for discipline in our lives and our church.

II. SECOND, THE GOSPEL ACCORDING TO "HOOSIERS" ILLUSTRATES THE NEED FOR A SECOND CHANCE.

A second character in the movie was "Shooter," the alcoholic father of one of the players on the team. He was a former player himself, whose knowledge of the game was obscured by his alcoholic binges bringing shame to his son and disrespect from the community. In a shocking reversal, Coach Dale asked "Shooter" to become his assistant coach, on the condition that he clean himself up, and remain sober in front of the boys. He offered him a second chance. He offered him a chance to redeem himself in the eyes of his son. The Gospel According to Hoosiers reminds us that we all need a second chance.

The Scriptures say, "All have sinned and fallen short of the glory of God." Why then do we have such a hard time offering forgiveness to those who have made mistakes and want to "Start over?" Maybe the reason Coach Dale was willing to offer "Shooter" a second chance was the fact that he too had been given a second chance. Like a well known coach from Ohio he had struck a player in a moment of rage, and had been banned from coaching in the state of New York.

Most people have something in their past that they would just as soon not have everyone know about. It seldom serves any purpose to label someone because they made a mistake in judgment twenty years ago. People can and do change. We need to give people a second chance. The scripture says, "Judge not that you be not judged" (Luke 6:37). The romantic interest in the movie involved another teacher, who "knew" something about Coach Dale's past, was tempted to use it, then withheld judgment, eventually began to support him, and finally fell in love.

She gave him a "second chance" and eventually began to look at him in a new light. It would make a lot of difference if we would begin to act differently toward people we didn't like. If we **act** differently toward them, we might begin to **feel** differently toward them.

The Gospel According to Hoosiers illustrates the need to give others a second chance.

III. THIRD, THE GOSPEL ACCORDING TO "HOOSIERS" ILLUSTRATES THE NEED TO BE THE BEST WE CAN BE.

We put too much emphasis on winning in our society. It's true that the movie "*Hoosiers*" is about winning the State Championship. But it is more than that. It is about people living up to their potential. It is about being the best you can be. I think that people are judged far more seriously by God for not living up to their potential than they are for winning or losing.

Remember the parable of the talents. Jesus' harshest words were for the servant who went out and buried his talent. He realized that there are one talent, two talent, and five talent people. They were not judged by how many talents they had, but by what they did with what they had.

I like the story about President Kennedy who was addressing a group of scientists, Nobel prize winners, and other dignitaries in the Blue Room of the White House. He said, "There is more talent and intellect gathered in this room tonight than ever before in the history of the country, with the one possible exception of the time Thomas Jefferson dined here alone." Of course, we're not Thomas Jeffersons, but we are who God has called us to be and we need to use the gifts God has given us for God's glory.

When the movie opened, there was one boy on the team who was too short, and as he said of himself, "I ain't no good." Yet Coach Dale believed in him and when the chips were down in a Regional game, he made the winning free throws. Coach Dale got him to believe in himself and when he did that the results spoke for themselves. I think Robert Schuller is right in suggesting that

Self-Esteem is the greatest need in our society right now, and that includes the Church. "Self-esteem is the human hunger for the divine that God intended to be our emotional birthright as Children created in His image. (*Self-Esteem, The New Reformation*, p.15).

A recent Gallup poll concluded that people with a strong sense of self-esteem have a high moral and ethical sensitivity, they have a strong sense of family, they are far more successful in inter-personal relationships, they are far more productive on the job, they are far lower in incidents of chemical addictions, they are more involved in social and political activities in their community, and they are far more generous to charitable institutions and relief causes.

One of the great challenges of the Church is to help people build their self-esteem and help them to be the best they can be, to live up to the potential which God has given them.

The Gospel According to Hoosiers illustrates our need for discipline, our need for a second chance, and our need to be the best we can be. It is a modern day morality play which concludes with Coach Dale saying "I love you guys." "Unconditional love is the most powerful healing force in the world." In playing the game of basketball we are reminded of another athlete who played the game of life--The Apostle Paul. "I have fought the good fight, I have finished the race, I have kept the faith. Henceforth there is laid up for me the crown of righteousness which the Lord, the righteous judge, will award to me on that Day, and not only to me but also to all who have loved his appearing." (II Timothy 4:7-8).

"When that last great Scorer comes to write against your name,
He writes not that you won or lost, but how you played the game."

CHAPTER FIVE
I PLANTED A GARDEN

I Corinthians 3:6

"I planted the seed, Apollos watered the plant, but it was God who made the plant grow."

Several years ago I planted a garden on some borrowed ground at Roy Easton's. Roy said one of his tenants had left a space and I could plant whatever I wanted. I planted the garden with the usual corn and beans. Then came tomatoes and potatoes. There were radishes, lettuce, carrots, and beets. I put in cucumbers, pumpkin, watermelon, and cantaloupe. There were butternut and acorn squash, onions and even okra. A row of zinnias and marigold completed the garden.

Well, the watermelon and cantaloupe didn't develop, but the beans, tomatoes, and radishes did fine. There were so many zucchini that people got tired of seeing me coming. You know how to tell a person in Indiana who doesn't have any friends? She's the only one at the supermarket buying zucchini!

The idea for this sermon came to me while I was planting early onions on Good Friday after I had learned of our move to Warsaw. Now other ministers might have been tempted to let the garden go; to forget the weeds; and not thin out the beets and carrots. But I am determined to finish something once I have started. When so much preparation and cultivation has taken place, not to reap a good harvest would be a shame.

Now I did not originate the analogy of planting a garden. The Apostle Paul, writing of the Church at Corinth said, "I planted, Apollos watered, but Got gave the increase." That is the way I would like you to think about our work with this congregation.

When the call came to consider coming to First Church I was not ready to leave South Bend Grace. When I was told that it would be a challenge, that piqued my interest, despite the fact that our boys were Juniors and Seniors at South Bend Riley. Nancy would leave yet another teaching job, with no certainty of finding another. Yet we came. The rest is history. We have come to love this congregation with an even greater depth of feeling than we thought was possible. For Nancy and Geoff and Kevin this has been our home. I want to thank you for making them a part of your family.

The congregation has grown steadily, not just numerically or financially, but spiritually. But I must say that I do not believe that the full potential has yet been realized. Like Moses who led his people up out of the wilderness but could not take them into the promised land, so we have come thus far with you. I do not doubt that you will get to the promised land. But I will not be able to go there with you. Other leadership will be required to fulfill your creative mission in this community. Like Paul, we have planted, but like his successor another gardener is coming to water or nourish the congregation into full maturity. Let him do it! He will be your pastor and should be asked to perform all pastoral tasks. I have known your new minister for many years and commend him to you with great confidence. The leadership of the congregation should assume even greater responsibility for carrying out the mission of the church. The future of the church depends upon it!

The church is not the extension of one person's personality or ambition or drive. "The Church is of God and will be preserved until the end of time, for the conduct of worship and the due administration of the Sacraments." That statement from the old membership liturgy reminds us all whose Church it is.

The Apostle wrote, "Who is Apollos, and who is Paul? We are simply God's servants, by whom you were led to believe." So it is with us. "The one who plants and the one who waters really do not matter. It is God who matters: for He makes the plant grow." It is God's Church.

I have been privileged to live among you as one who serves. For what is a minister but a servant? Your servant and God's servant! The root meaning of the word "minister" means "one who serves." We have shared your grief and disappointments; rejoiced with you in your happy occasions; we have baptized your infants, confirmed your children, married your young adults, counseled with those in trouble, and buried your dead. We have tried to organize you for mission, and equip you for your ministry to others. This is the highest honor you can bestow upon another person--to allow them to be your minister.

Dr. Carroll Wise, my teacher of Pastoral Care at Garrett has written: "Our ministry is not 'our' ministry, but the continuation of Christ's ministry in us through his Spirit...The temptation in the ministry to work our various ego needs...is very subtle, extensive, and potent...One way for the pastor to deal with this problem in himself is through the constant reminder that the ministry is not one's private affair but is the ministry of Christ through him/her...It is in this spirit that the true pastor fills his/her calling." (*The Meaning of Pastoral Care*, p. 7).

Paul said, "I planted, but Apollos watered." Paul moved on, but he never forgot his former congregation. It should be a self-evident truth that we will not forget this congregation. How could we? Can a father forget his son; a mother her daughter? No more could we forget you. We will pray for you. And we will pray for your new pastor and his wife as they come to live and serve among you. We ask you to show them the same kindness you have shown to us. They will bring experience and skills that we did not have. The congregation needs what they have to offer. Allow them to minister in your midst.

In my garden at Roy's place I made a couple of mistakes. I planted some of the rows too far apart and spent considerably more time than I should have cultivating weeds. I let some weeds grow that should have been cut out. And then there were some plants that were put too close together. I had forgotten how far squash and cucumbers spread. People, like plants--need proper growing space. We need to take care that there is room to grow. In this regard proper planning is required. The congregation must implement the Long Range Plan on the future of the Church. I remind you again of the advice of one of my Chinese friends:

> 1. In the long range future you look for growth. Look for the potential!
>
> 2. In the intermediate future you look to take a calculated risk.
>
> 3. At the present time you meet the demands.

Whereas one planted, another has come to water and nourish. But we must never forget that it is God who makes the plant grow.

I can only give God the credit for the growth of this church. His spirit has been at work in our midst. I believe that it is God's purpose that his church continue to grow. But He cannot do it alone! "God has no hands but our hands to do His work today; He has no feet but our feet, to spread His work on its way." We are creative partners in this work. There is an old story about a crusty old agnostic who was working in his garden one day when a pious Christian came by, and trying to shake his agnosticism said, "That's quite a garden you and God have there." The agnostic thought a minute, then said, "You should have seen it when God had it all to himself." Perhaps he said more than he knew.

In "Choruses from 'The Rock,'" T.S. Eliot wrote:
And the church must be forever building, and always
  decaying and always being restored...
And all that is ill you may repair if you walk together
  in humble repentance...
And all that was good you must fight to keep with hearts
  as devoted as those of your fathers who fought to gain it."

Today is the last Sunday of the Christian Year. Next Sunday is the First Sunday of Advent. What better time to talk about drawing to a close the work of eleven years, and to look forward to new beginnings than with Advent as we dream about the future.

We all had dreams and visions once upon a time. Remember when you used to dream about how it was going to be when you would finally be a teenager, when you finally got your driver's license, when you graduated from high school, when you would be 21, when you got married, had kids, retired. What will it be like when...? What would it be like if...?

As a runner, one such dream kept me going. Every run was a marathon. I must have won the Olympics 15 times, and the Boston Marathon 20 times. But I know that was a fantasy rather than a dream, but it sustained me on those particularly cold days when the wind was blowing and I was tired to begin with.

And I've had dreams and visions for this church, but with

a difference. Those dreams and visions became possible, because they did not depend on the strength of my legs, or mind or spirit, but they were born out of the promise and purpose of God. I'm lucky, because I participated in the realization of those dreams.

I — we — had a dream of a church alive and moving and growing, but for its own sake, but in commitment and love and faith and stewardship, and excitement. Of a church making a difference in our community and our conference and maybe even in the world. Of a church alive and well, serving the people of this community, and being witnesses, because we have been there from the beginning.

As you come to the end of your current Visions in Action there are two projects you need to consider. One is the chapel and the other is the bell tower. The first because it is needed and the second because it will be beautiful. Both were a part of the original architectural design. Finish the church as it was meant to be.

The Church has a dream expressed in the early prayers of the Church, when it said, "Thy kingdom come, O Lord," and when it proclaimed, "Even so, Come Lord Jesus."

All over Christendom there is talk of the need for renewal of the Church. It is said that what we need is a "new" Church. The Church that needs renewal is the human manifestation of HIS Church. The women and men who are being built into God's church are still in need of growth and development as they move on to maturity in Christ. From this point of view the Church does need renewal.

G. K. Chesterton once wrote: "The Christian ideal has not been tried and found wanting; it has been found difficult and left untried." This is the future goal toward which we move. Our goal is the "Renewed" Church that is in the process of becoming.

In a recent graduation on a large state university campus, the president shook hands individually with every member of the graduating class. He said the same thing to each person: "Congratulations, and keep moving." Those of us who have attended those functions know why he said those words. But there is a deeper meaning here. To the members of First Church we say: "Congratulations, and keep moving." And may the God of peace go with you.

CHAPTER SIX

GARAGE SALE THEOLOGY AND OTHER MOVING EXPERIENCES

Luke 7:36:8-3

A garage sale can be a religious experience. We've been through enough of them to know. Our most recent three day sale was a case in point. You meet the nicest and most interesting people at garage sales. Let me tell you about some of the people I met last week.

First, there was Debbie. (That's not her real name). Debbie was standing at the table for checking out when I walked up with an armload of books. Her mother was standing with her. She had a strained look on her face like she had been through unbearable pain. I asked, "Would you be interested in any of these books?" She asked, "What kind of books are they?" "Oh," I said, "some are religious books, some dealing with life's problems," sensing her discomfort. She came over to the book table and began to pour out her pain. "My son was just killed by a drunk driver in Bloomington. He was an honor student, and was in his senior year. Would you like to see a picture of him?" Thus began a long counseling session in which she shared her grief and sorrow. I told her of some friends of mine who had lost a son the same age; I referred her to two books. One by John Claypool, *Tracks of a Fellow Struggler*, and *Lament for a Son*, by a Dutch theologian whose son was killed in a mountain climbing accident.

She seemed relieved to have someone to talk to. Her big concern was the fact that the girl who killed her son was going to prison for three years. She had tried to get it reduced and testified on behalf of the girl. In that encounter, I discovered pain and grief, grace and forgiveness all coalesced into one beautiful experience of Christian sharing.

She said, "We're Episcopalians. But I've always found

that someone always comes by, just when you need them. I knew that you were sent by God the moment you walked up here." They paid for the desk and carpet and I gave her my card with the names of the books on it. I doubt if I will ever see her again, but I will never forget her and will remember this "Garage Sale Pilgrim" for as long as I live.

Yet another Garage Sale Pilgrim came to our sale, not once but several times. As we unpacked items, new treasures emerged to encourage new customers. After about five trips to pick up an assortment of tape recorders, and radios which he fixes up, this obviously brilliant man stood for the longest time in the driveway and finally said, "You're a minister. There is something I've been wanting to ask you." I have learned over the years that when that comment is made, usually there is a statement disguised as a question coming, often not very complimentary. I wasn't disappointed. "It seems to me," he said, "that religion is losing its influence in our world. Things seem to be going from bad to worse. There aren't heros anymore, anybody you can look up to. The Church I grew up in (Roman Catholic) you always admired the priest. But now I don't know."

"Well," I said, "I have to agree with you. It does seem that religion has come through some hard times recently. The television evangelists' scandals, the linking of religious fanaticism with resurgent nationalism as in Iran, the moral lapses that people are always so quick to point out when a brother or sister falls, there is plenty of evidence to point to a diminishing influence. But look at the other side. Did you ever think what kind of shape we'd be in without it? Remember what the scriptures say: 'We have these treasures in earthen vessels.' Our faith is in God, not in God's messengers. Scripture tells us that when a brother or sister falls, it is our duty to pick them up and restore them to a right relationship. We still believe in the Gospel of the Second Chance."

I reminded him of the medieval manuscript someone found which read, "The Church is like Noah's ark, if it weren't for the storm on the outside, you couldn't stand the smell on the inside." The Church has survived for two thousand years and we believe "The Church is of God and will be preserved until the end of time..." Besides, I'm more encouraged today than I was several years ago when the Jesus movement was sweeping people out of organized religion. But it didn't last, because it wasn't built on a solid foundation. I believe there is a resurgence of interest among the young people, especially young families in the so-called "Baby Boomer" generation who are returning to the Church in large numbers because they sense something fundamentally sound in the Church's message. We must not disappoint them.

He left saying he was glad he had talked to me. He'd been thinking about this for a long time and hadn't had any one to discuss it with. He'd think about what I told him and thanked me for my time. I said, "Anytime!" Maybe at our next Garage Sale we would meet again and we could compare notes on how the Church is doing or not doing in our world.

I was reminded of our lesson from last week. . ."Always be ready to make a defense to any one who calls you to account for the hope that is in you." (I Peter 3:15)

That is something we do every day of our lives, in our office, our classroom, with our relatives, and the people in our neighborhood. In seminary we called it Christian Apologetics. For most of us, it is simply Christian witnessing. "Always be ready to make a defense. . ."

My third Garage Sale Encounter came toward the end of the sale. It was late in the afternoon and a middle aged couple came to the door. They picked up a few items and we got to talking about movies and values for today's children and suddenly he looked at my fishing rods stacked in a corner and asked, "Don't you have something to hang the rods from by their tips?" I said I didn't and she looked at him knowingly and said, "Why don't you go out to the car and get him one of your fish." Without a word he disappeared and presented me with a wooden fish with notches in it for hanging rods from their tips. I said, "This is beautiful, how much do you want for it?" "Nothing," he said, "I'm a retired carpenter and I make these for a hobby to give to people. You see, I'm on total disability. Several years ago I had a brain tumor about this big, and it left me unable to work." "Well, at least let me give you these items for free," I said. He refused.

He went on to explain that when he was ill, the doctors told him he would never walk again. His Church began to pray for him and for his recovery. And today, though disabled, he makes a ministry of sharing his skills with people who need them, like me. You can bet that my fishing rods will hang straight and secure from now on. And I will think about Ed every time I go fishing. But more than that, I will think about the power of prayer and the effectiveness of that simple witness every time I head for the lake or river or farm pond.

He turned his pain into power, his misfortune into adventure, his weakness into strength. This is one "Garage Sale Pilgrim" who will remain in my mind forever.

In the award-winning movie *Chariots of Fire*, the Scottish runner, Eric Liddel, asks the question, "From where do we get the strength to run to the finish?" He answers, "It comes from within."

Inner strength flows like an underground stream through the Bible. It took a while for the stream of strength to go underground; up until about the time of Elijah, the God of the Old Testament seemed to roar like a raging river. Strength was equated with armies and numbers, but with Elijah and subsequent prophets, the still, small voice of God began to be heard and the superior strength of the meek and quiet people like Ed began to be recognized. It was Paul's "Christ within" strength which far outlasted the might of the Roman Empire. The psalmist repeatedly stated "The Lord is my strength..the Lord is the strength of my life."

Do you feel the quiet inward strength flowing through today's Psalm used in the Call to Worship? "As a hart (deer) longs for flowing streams, so longs my soul for thee, O God. My soul thirsts for God, for the living God...Why are you cast down, O my soul, and why are you disquieted within me? Hope in God; for I shall again praise him, my help and my God." (Ps. 42:1-2,11).

In our new Hymnal there is a hymn from my childhood, "Near to the Heart of God" which begins "There is a place of quiet rest, near to the heart of God; a place where sin cannot molest, near to the heart of God."

Well, the Garage Sale ended and moving day was upon us. I ended up taking one of the movers to the hospital after he had snapped something in his back trying to lift our TV.

The move to our new house was one I will not soon forget. Thanks to three of our members we had trucks to move the boxes and unsold Garage Sale items that we had not put in the Trash to Treasure Sale here at the Church. It was one of the truck trips that provided the most memorable experience of the day. It was raining so I threw a long indoor-outdoor carpet over the boxes to protect them from the rain. Almost as an after thought I decided to "anchor" the carpet with an old wooden box which had my lifetime collection of baseballs and softballs in it. When I arrived at the house I discovered that the box was gone and so were the baseballs and softballs.

In about fifteen minutes up drove Mark Russell with a battered and bruised box and what was left of the balls. He had come upon the box in the middle of the road, and then had noticed an assortment of baseballs and softballs strewn over the Purdue Golf Course. He put two and two together and redeemed the situation by picking up all the balls he could find and putting them back in the box. We had a good laugh and then I said, "How biblical." Finding the lost and restoring them to their former owner.

That is the task of the church. There are several stories in the New Testament which deal with the lost sheep, the lost coin, and the lost son. In each case the lost is found, and there is great rejoicing. Such was the case in our moving experience. I signed one of the balls and gave it to his son, Matthew, who is a Little Leaguer. Some day he will appreciate the theology of this moving experience. The Bible is full of other stories with moving experiences. The people of Israel were a people on the move. Their journey toward the Promised Land is but a prototype of our own pilgrimage. We too are a pilgrim people. Always on the move, and certain that God will be with us in all our moving experiences.

Now, I suspect you think I've been talking about books, fishing poles, and baseballs. I've really been talking about grace and forgiveness, commitment and redemption. Whatever theology you live by and whatever moving experiences you have, I hope you will find God in them, for you have already been found by God.

CHAPTER SEVEN
A LETTER FROM HOME

II Timothy 1:1-14

There is nothing quite so welcome as a letter from home. When one is separated from loved ones by geography nothing stirs the imagination so much as a word from familiar surroundings. Even when the news is bad we are glad to keep "in touch" with what is going on back home.

This is the theme of Paul's Epistle to Timothy. Timothy was Paul's son in the faith . . . now a co-worker. Paul's object in writing is to inspire and strengthen Timothy for his task in Ephesus. Timothy was young and he had a hard task in battling against the heresies and the infections that were bound to threaten the Church. So, then, in order to keep his courage high and his effort strenuous, Paul reminds Timothy of certain things.

(1) He reminds him of his own confidence in him. There is no greater inspiration than to feel that someone believes in us. An appeal to honor is always more effective than a threat of punishment. The fear of letting down those who love us is a cleansing thing.

(2) He reminds him of his family tradition. Timothy was walking in a fine heritage, and if he failed, not only would he smirch his own name, but he would lessen the honor of his family name as well. A fine parentage is one of the greatest gifts a person can have. Let us thank God for it and never bring dishonor to it. Not only are we part of a biological family but also we belong to the church family . . . the family of God. The family meal that we shall partake with millions of Christians today is a reminder that we have One Faith, One Hope, One Lord, One God.

To our students here this morning we remind you that there are those persons back home who are thinking of you and praying for you at this very moment. Sometimes a thoughtful and articulate parent will put into print words that help very much at the time and when read later help even more. The following letter was received by a friend of mine from his father when he was starting his college career years ago and I have his permission to share it with you.

Dear Son:

    I am writing you this letter because there are some things I want to tell you that I knew you would never remember if I told you here at home. You have left home now and it will never be the same for you again, for you have taken the first step on the long road to becoming a man. Growing up is not easy. With the joy of new freedom and independence comes the harsh reality of making life decisions and suffering the consequences. You will soon face this in your social life at school. There were certain standards established for you here at our parsonage home that pretty well defined the scope of your social life. The only standards you will have now are those you choose yourself. I hope you will choose wisely.

    You will soon encounter that strange breed of persons called professors. They come in assorted sizes and colors and all are reputed to be ogres to some degree. Get acquainted with them. You will find them to be helpful, good, and kind. And, then, I harbor some fond hope that they may teach you something. You will find at least one professor who considers it his sacred duty to destroy your faith in God. Don't be too alarmed about this. First, your faith ought to be tested or it is never going to be strong. And if it can't stand testing, it isn't worthy of being your faith. Then remember, God has survived our doubts for a long, long time now, and my latest word is that he is doing quite well. Most real people who have faced much of life have found a living faith in God. I hope you will attend church, now that you are away from home and no longer have to go to church. Don't be too discouraged by the preaching you hear. Most university ministers are notoriously poor preachers. (Editorial note: Please bear in mind this was written a good many years ago). Remember, you go to church to worship God, and this you can do, even with a poor sermon.

Before very long I am afraid you will meet the problem of evil and the problem of sin, head-on. No textbook can be of much help here. I strongly recommend you try prayer. I will close now with this reminder: You are twice loved. Your mother and I love you with all our hearts and we're proud of you. Keep us that way. Last but by far the most important, God loves you. May He always be proud of you.

Dad

The writer of that letter was named Phillips Brooks Smith, Sr. His son, Phillips Brooks Smith, Jr. or "P.B." was your former pastor and my friend. Although it was not my privilege to know Phillips Sr., I knew his wife and attended her memorial service last year. Those who knew Dr. Smith attest to his loving quality of life. That letter from home was never forgotten by that son, who became the District Superintendent of the Huntington District. It will stay with him and the people he has shared it with for many generations.

In his letter to Timothy, Paul reminded him of his setting apart to office and of the gift which was conferred upon him. Once a person enters upon the service of any association with a tradition, anything that he does affects not only himself/herself nor has it to be done only on his/her strength. There is the strength of a tradition to draw upon and the honor of a tradition to preserve. That is especially true of the Church. Those who serve it have its honor in their hands; those who serve it are strengthened by the consciousness of the communion of all the saints.

One of those saints, now a part of the church triumphant, I did have the privilege of knowing. Her name was Helen Palmer. I held her memorial service last year. She was a person of quiet dignity and positive faith, despite the fact that she witnessed the tragic death of her husband, a son and a son-in-law. She wrote this letter to her daughter at Purdue in 1940.

My dear Georgia:

I do wish you wouldn't be so scared about those exams. I'm sure you can get through them some way but if you can't we love you just the same. You know a brave person is not one who is not afraid but one who goes ahead even though he is terribly afraid. So I really do think you have a great deal of courage. Read the ninety-first Psalm. The one that starts "He that dwelleth in the secret place of the most High shall abide under the shadow of the Almighty." Read the first twelve verses, I'm sure it will help you. Then read the Hundred Twenty First Psalm. It starts "I will lift up mine eyes unto the hills, from whence cometh my help." Read them and really believe them for they are real. That poetry wouldn't have lasted all these years if it hadn't been able to strengthen those who were afraid and needed help. God is in those verses and is ready and able to help you if you will but calmly trust him. Of course, you can study and do your part but you do not need to have that panic and fear in your heart and you do not need to sit up nights studying when you need your rest more than you do the studying. You have studied as well as you could, now you do not need to be afraid. There is so much material to cover that you can not possibly go over it all minutely, so do what you can, and have confidence in yourself and faith in God who will help you to be calm and use those powers and abilities which you already possess.

Love,
Mother

P.S. Read one of those chapters every night. I am praying for you.

    Is there any doubt in your mind that that girl did graduate from Purdue. She went on to become a master teacher. She is in her own right . . . a saint.

    These letters from home remind us of the qualities which should characterize the Christian person and teacher. In the letter to Timothy, Paul outlined four of these qualities.

    (a) There was courage. It was not craven fear but courage that Christian service should bring to a person. It always takes courage to be a Christian, and that courage comes from the continual consciousness of the presence of Christ.

(b) There was power. In the true Christian there is the power to cope, the power to shoulder the back-breaking task, the power to stand erect in the face of the shattering situation, the power to retain faith in the face of the soul-searing sorrow and the wounding disappointment. The Christian is characteristically the person who could pass the breaking point and not break.

(c) There was love. In Timothy's case this was love for the brethren, for the congregation of the people of Christ over whom he was set. It is precisely that love that motivated Phillips Brooks Smith, Sr. and Helen Palmer to write to their children at school. Letters full of challenge, hope and love.

(d) There was self-discipline. The word is **sophronismos**, one of those great Greek untranslatable words. Someone has defined it as "the sanity of saintliness." Another says it is "control of oneself in the face of panic or of passion." It is Christ alone who can give us that self-mastery which will keep us alike from being swept away and from running away. No one can effectively teach/learn until he/she has first mastered himself/herself.

So this morning, whether we are receiving or sending letters from home, let us not be ashamed to say, "I know whom I have believed, and I am sure that he is able to guard until that Day what has been entrusted to me." II. Tim. 1:12.

CHAPTER EIGHT
WORSHIP AND THE THEATRE

Isaiah 6:1-8
Acts 2:42

"And they devoted themselves to...the prayers. When Ernest Fremont Tittle was pastor of First Methodist Church, Evanston, Illinois, people would regularly phone the church office and ask, "Is Dr. Tittle preaching next Sunday?" To which the secretary (primed for the question) would answer: "No, but we plan to worship God just the same."

There needs to be a drastic revision in our attitude toward worship. This can be seen in the one layman of one church who always entered the sanctuary just prior to the sermon. When asked why he was always late, he answered: "I'm not interested in the preliminaries." Maybe the problem is that too many people feel like mere spectators to religious exercises being performed by specialists.

The 100 year old illustration of Soren Kierkegaard is still very helpful to people in interpreting their place in corporate worship. He pointed out that many nominal Protestants see themselves as the critical audience, where the preacher is the actor whose art they are expected to enjoy. The truth is, he reminded us all, the worshipers are the actors, God is the audience, and the minister is only the prompter reminding them of their lines, and whispering the text by which the people may examine themselves before the living God. Well, it would make a lot of difference if we remembered that.

We call ours a "service of worship." Service! We ought to be ashamed of ourselves. That's what Ruskin thought, anyway. What colossal nerve, he said, those Christians have to use a word like service, a word with blood, sweat, and tears in it, with muscle and sinew in it to denote those sedate gatherings at which they simply sit and think...and sometimes only sit.

Worship, for those who do not already know, follows a natural progression. The classic example of movement in worship is Isaiah 6. First there is **Vision**--"I saw the Lord." An encounter with God brings **Humility**--"Woe is me...for I am a man of unclean lips." Then with the symbolic cleansing **Vitality** is given..."Behold, this has touched your lips, your guilt is taken away, and your sin is forgiven." With forgiveness comes **Illumination**--"I heard the voice of the Lord." The appropriate response to God's word is always **Dedication**--"Here I am! Send me." Vision--Humility--Vitality--Illumination--Dedication--and Peace.

Perhaps you've noticed that we follow a pattern of worship too. There aren't many Sundays when you have in your hands an outline of the morning sermon that you can take home with you to enlighten the physically and spiritually "sleepy ones." Hopefully, by looking at this order of worship we can avoid the misunderstanding that at worship we are to be entertained; and learn instead, how we ought to participate.

The introduction to the order of worship sets the tone for that which follows: "Worship begins with the first note of the organ. Bow in silent meditation upon entering the sanctuary and prepare to meet with God in communion and worship."

I. **The Adoration of God.**

Worship begins with adoration and praise. A traveler in India once heard loud drum beats coming from a temple and was told in explanation, "the priests are waking up the god. It's almost time for worship." Christians do not worship a God who needs arousing. Christians worship God so that he can awaken them. We sing the hymn, "He that keepeth Israel, slumbers not nor sleeps." Would to God that could be said of every member of the congregation. We are aware of the different stages of spiritual slumber when we ask God to "Comfort the afflicted and afflict the comfortable."

Martin Buber had a wonderful word on worship: "God cannot be expressed, he can only be addressed," which is a continual reminder that the final depths of the Christian life are not realized in the brilliancy of our thinking, but in the maturity of our prayer and worship.

Again, let us remember God is not the object of our worship but **rather the subject**; the one who elicits and calls forth the giving of ourselves to Him. This begins with the prelude, (which is not a performance, but an aid to meditation) and concludes with the hymn of praise and prayer of invocation. The selection of hymns always seeks to fit in with the theme for the morning, for the service is a unit.

I am often asked "why don't we sing more of those "oldies, but goodies." If they mean the hymns of the 1st and 2nd centuries or the great Reformation hymns of the 16th century I reply, "Fine, what would you like to suggest?" But if they mean the post-Wesley, 19th century, "rhythm-n-blues" swingers, which are long on the feelings but short on theology; then I want to ask, "What is it you like about this hymn." Invariably the reply comes back, "they make me feel good." Now I grew up in this tradition, and I felt good right along with the others, but about what, I couldn't tell you. I didn't look at the words, either. We didn't sing hymns like "A Mighty Fortress is our God" which as Charles Smith in his controversial book *How to Become Bishop Without Being Religious*, suggests (with tongue-in-cheek) is really one of the poorer hymns of the church. It is too majestic; it stresses the greatness of God, his power and majesty. It gives all the attention to God and praises Him--but none to humans. And furthermore it isn't sentimental; it doesn't swing-n-sway or bounce. Whereas, those "old" hymns emphasize the importance of humanity. Did you ever notice in a typical Fanny Crosby hymn how many times the pronouns "I", or "me" and "mine" are used? Look it up sometime.

The point of all this is that worship cannot center solely on ourselves. It must begin with God as we declare his worth. For this is what worship actually means--"worth-ship." We declare God's worth. Then after we have approached God, as did Isaiah, we are brought, like the young prophet, to the necessity of confession.

II. **The Confession to God.**

The very mention of the word "confession" stirs up the imagination of many all of the misconceptions which have accompanied the Roman Catholic practice of Confession. There have been, it is true, certain abuses throughout the history of the church. But the reformers certainly didn't intend to do away with the confessional in their new structure. The need for us to confess our sin was best summarized by our father in the faith, John Wesley: "And if any of you should at any time fall from what you now are, if you should again feel delivered, do not deny, do not hide, do not disguise it at all, at the peril of your soul. At all events go to one in whom you can confide, and speak just what you feel. God will enable him to speak a word in season, which shall be health to your soul. And surely he will again lift up your head, and cause the bones that have been broken to rejoice." (Christian Perfection). Confession is not only theologically valid, it is medically sound. A bad conscience can, over a period of years so strangle a person's life that his physical and mental powers of resistance are thereby impaired. It can be the root cause of certain illnesses. It is like a stopper which can be pulled out by confession, so that life begins at once to flow again. There can be no forgiveness without confession. No cheap grace. Then when we have cleansed our soul we are ready to affirm our faith. Jesus Christ, our brother has promised forgiveness of sin to all who will receive it!

 III. **Affirmation of Faith.**

 Affirmation of faith begins with the creed. The root meaning of this word is credo, "I believe"; the first two words of the Apostle's Creed. We're so used to saying what we don't believe, that it is a good discipline for us to affirm positively what we **do** believe. The various creeds (or "rules of faith"), the scriptures, and the pastoral prayers affirm our faith in God, reveal His word, and seek His guidance. In all of this we are participants.

 Now it is true that one's creed is not one's religion, any more than one's backbone is the person. But a good backbone is a very essential part of our religion. We still hear it said occasionally that "it makes no difference what a person believes, so long as he or she is sincere..."

 Recently, in a *Peanuts* cartoon strip, Linus confided to Charlie Brown, that he wanted to be a prophet when he grew up. Charlie Brown said that was nice, but prophets almost always turned out to be false prophets. To which Linus replied, "Perhaps I could be a sincere false prophet!" Sincerity! It does not make any difference what we believe so long as we are "sincere" about it! We are told we should not criticize the idea of a presidential candidate because he is so "sincere" his defenders apparently equating "sincerity" with truth and not realizing the candidate could well be sincerely wrong. A traveler takes the wrong train; going north, sincerely believing it to be the southbound train. Will it make no difference? "You are what you believe." Our age needs a positive, affirmative note. In worship we affirm our faith. Then from affirmation we lead naturally to dedication.

IV. **Dedication of Life.**

The basic question to the young prophet Isaiah was, "whom shall I send and who will go for me." The response then, and now, is in the text: "Here I am, send me." Yet all too often the response of the church member is "Here I am, send **him**, send **her**." The dedication of life is like an Indian prince who gave his queen a valuable diamond. Later on a tour he stopped in England and during his audience he asked to see the diamond. It was brought and he held it in his hand and saw again its beauty and realized its value, but he said, "Again, I give it to you."

Dedication is not a thing done once and then it is all over. It must be done again and again. It must be done each day. Basic to the dedication of life is the offertory service. The very phrase itself is illustrative of self-giving. "Offering"--a concrete expression of part of one's expended time. We have recently placed the offering after the sermon in the order of worship. We do this for two reasons. One, because historically in the early church this was where it belonged; and second, because it is a vital part of the dedication of life.

Adoration, confession, affirmation, dedication; this is the pattern of our worship. We come not to be entertained, but to participate. We cannot participate if we are not present.

Faithfulness at worship services nurtures the soul, encourages other people, and honors Him who is the Head of the Church. Many people suffer "the slings and arrows of outrageous fortune" and then lose their faith. The soul was already dead--the storm only revealed that fact. People don't lose faith and lose heart because of what happens to them. When their souls have already died of neglect, they're a pushover for any tough break life sends their way. Renewal of spirit, deepening of trust, developing of spiritual resources, honoring of Christ, these take place in worship. Whoever says Jesus Christ is Savior and Lord will get the body to church.

The people who risked their lives and climbed over smoking rubble to get into London's churches during the worst of World War II were responding to the love of God in Christ as Christians have done all through the ages. Despite the edicts of Roman emperors and exposure to inhuman tortures the early Christians came together for worship, and we hear of the same determination among Baptists meeting on back streets in Russia today. Worship is and always will be one of the major activities of the Christian church. It is one of the "marks of the church."

"And they devoted themselves to the prayers." The call to be a Christian disciple is a call to fellowship, and a call to worship.

CHAPTER NINE
WHAT KEEPS US LISTENING?

John 1:14A

J.   What this country needs is a good five-cent cigar.

P.   I say, "live by the Golden Rule."

J.   When better cars are built, Buick will build them.

P.   I'm not prejudiced. I just wouldn't want to live next door to one.

J.   Prejudice--the Golden Rule

P.   Sin-Salvation

J.   Hermeneutics--Homiletics

P.   Is it true--Is it exegetically responsible?

J.   Paradoxical.

P.   Expansive

J.   I hear you saying...

P.   Do you mean to say...

J.   Words

P.   Words

          (PAUSE)

J.   Silence

P. Silence--what does it mean?

J. Words--what do they mean?

P. Nothing

J. Something

P. Let's talk about words

J. Let's talk about silence

P. Words, word, The Word. "For Heaven's Sake," that's right. That reminds me, "The Word."

J. "The Word" -- I know it

J. I open my mouth to speak
and the word is there,
Formed by the lips, the tongue,
The organ of voice. Formed by
The brain, transmitting the word
By breath.

I open my mouth to speak
And the word is there,
Traveling between us--caught
By the organ of hearing, the ear,
Transmitting the thought to the brain
Through the word.

Just so do we communicate--
You and I: the thought
From one mind leaping to another,
Given shape and form and substance,
So that we know and are known
Through the word.

P.   But let me speak to my very small son
And the words mean nothing,
For he does not know my language.
And so I must show him: "This is your foot,"
I say; "and it is meant for walking."
I help him up: "Here is the way to walk:'
And one day "walking" shapes in his brain
With the word.

God had something to say to Man,
But the words meant nothing,
For we did not know his language.
And so we were shown: "Behold, the Man,"

He said, "This is the image, the thought
In my mind--Man as I mean him, loving and serving.
I have put Him in flesh. Now the Word
Has shape and form and substance
To travel between us. Let Him show forth love
Till one day 'loving' shapes in your brain
With the Word."

      (pp. 18-19) Baker's Plays, 100 Summer Street, Boston
                           Helen Kromer

J.   "And The Word Became Flesh and dwelt among us."..."So the word of God became a human being and lived among us." That's from John, the first chapter, the fourteenth verse.

P.   What does that mean to you,...and me...and them?

J.   For me it means that God speaks in human experience. I think this is what John was trying to say to his readers. God spoke in the man Jesus of Nazareth. That is to say He entered human history, our history, at a particular time and at a particular place.

P. It doesn't seem real that God could get mixed up with people.

J. That's what people were saying when the Gospel of John was written--God couldn't get involved in human affairs. God was high and holy and above us, removed from the grubby business of making a living and having kids.

P. You know--that's the way it seems to me--there are times when God seems so far away--

J. I know what you mean--it's as though God is silent.

P. Yes, silent. The silence of God is oppressive. I've tried devotions. I've read the books. (The Upper Room). There's no word in that for me.

J. I've had the same experience. I remember my family sitting down at the table and my father announcing, "This month we're going to have family devotions." And three days later, I say, "hey Dad, what happened to devotions?" Or I take the Bible out and say, "This week I'm going to read the Bible each day before I do anything else"---

P. You mean I'm not the only one...

J. You're not the only one.

P. I sometimes wonder...is it because I'm not listening...or God's not speaking.

I know there are times when I don't listen. I don't listen to other people. I just tune them out. I remember one day I was out calling for prospective members. At one home a young woman told me her grandfather is a Baptist minister. I thought, "she's no prospect; I'd better get on." Then she told me her grandmother had recently died. I sat there half-listening, professionally responding. But all the time I was thinking, "I've got to get on and find a prospect." That's the way I am with God. I've got to get on to something else. There's no time to listen.

J. But what happens when you do listen? When you try with all you've got to hear God speak. And there's nothing. No word. Only silence.

Last week I read the book, *Johnny Got His Gun*, by Dalton Trumbo. Johnny goes off to fight in the First World War and is a victim of a bomb explosion. He lives through the horror but finds himself transformed into a world of silence and darkness after losing his hearing, sight, ability to speak, and his arms and legs. His only tie to the world outside is his sense of touch. Using his head he manages to tap a message in Morse Code to a nurse and doctor, who translate its ferocity. He asks to be taken to places where governments meet so they can see---"this is war." He demands to be shown to children so they may see what happens when they go off to fight in wars. The only response Johnny gets from the doctor who returns the message by tapping on his chest is, "this request is against regulations! Who are you?" Johnny in despair returns to his own world again, allowing the chasm of silence to separate him from the world, war, and folly.

I, in a different sense, try to tap my message to God...

I try to communicate with God. In the Church I affirm the creeds; I pray the prayers; I eat the bread and drink the wine. And afterwards the silence.

P. For **us** the silence is real. Can we hear The Word?

"And the Word became flesh and dwelt among us." That's the way John said it in the first century. This is the way Helen Kromer says it in the Twentieth Century.

> God had something to say to Man,
> But the words meant nothing,
> For we did not know his language.
> And so we were shown: "Behold, the Man."

J.   Then Jesus is the word that breaks the silence of God. God spoke through the man Jesus of Nazareth to the people. It seemed strange to people in those days that God should come in such an unexpected way. They hardly could believe God was speaking in human experience. Some didn't believe and some don't today. Some did believe and some do believe today that God speaks in human experience in unexpected ways.

I recall one Sunday morning when I was visiting in a large city--new to me, that I went to a famous church expecting to hear God speak. The Gothic architecture was designed to inspire awe. The robed choir had rehearsed to sing praises. The preacher had prepared to speak a word for God. Yet I came away unmoved; there had been little communication for me. On the other hand, recently I attended the movie, "A Man for All Seasons." I went to the movie for entertainment and appreciation. But when the movie reached the climactic scene in which Sir Thomas Moore cupped his hands and said "when a man takes an oath, he holds himself in his hands, and he must watch lest he let himself spill through and drain away." That scene and those words struck me with great impact!

Strange that I came away from church that Sunday unmoved, and away from the theatre greatly moved. Now I recall that you have said that God speaks His word in strange places.

P.   Not only unexpected ways, but at the most unusual times.

One of the clearest words from God I have heard in recent years came not in the church, or in the study, but in a third-floor coffee house in Columbus, Ohio, called "The Cracked Cup." Four pastors with receding hairlines tried to join the college crowd and remain as inconspicuous as possible. A young man with a guitar went to the platform and sang a song for us, and the audience, and every person who stands before God: "Don't put me on, boy--I want you to be the real you." That was a good word--a needed word--an honest word to me--from God. I know in my bones that I can't "put Him on." And I want to be the "real me" in all of my relationships--here, and at home, and in my church. This is what I mean when I say that God speaks to us in human experience in unexpected ways. Thus we are never far from His Word--if we are open and responsive, we can hear Him in unpredictable places and at unusual times.

J. What have we said?

P. The Silence Is Real.

J. Jesus is the Word that breaks the Silence of God.

P. God speaks in human experience in unexpected ways.

J. What difference will this make in our lives?

P. What difference is it making now?

J. It keeps us listening.

P. And He Speaks To Us.

CHAPTER TEN

LEADERSHIP AND THE LION KING

Matthew 16:13-20

In the opening scene of the new Disney film, *The Lion King*, a new lion cub named Simba, is presented to the animal kingdom by his father, Mufasa, who is the King of the Beasts. All the animals bow in deference to the future leader of the animal kingdom. Before he is presented, he is marked on the forehead by Rafiki, the aged monkey, who serves the role of priest and shaman to the community. Throughout the film, the father reminds his young son, "Remember who you are." Remember who you are!

Just so you were held up at your Baptism and marked as special persons in the eyes of God and the community. You still are. Remember who you are and Whose you are!

I see three aspects of leadership in *The Lion King* which are instructive to us today. These three realities will help us focus on the message of the Gospel lesson from Matthew 16.

I. When your leadership is announced, someone close to you will betray you.

In the film, Simba's uncle, whose name was Scar, undermined Simba's future under the guise of love and concern. While pretending to give him advice and help, Scar was paving the way for the downfall of Mufasa and Simba and the realization of his own ambition to be the King of the Beasts. Simba trusted his uncle because he was "family" and nearly lost his future and his life.

One of Jesus' most trusted advisers was Judas, the treasurer. Surely Judas had won the respect and admiration of our Lord. His position was one of honor and leadership. Yet Judas suffered from a fatal flaw--ambition. He tried to force the issue and make Jesus a political Messiah. This was his Achilles' heel and because of it he lost his position and his life. Remember the words of St. John Chrysostom in the 4th century: "The road to Hell is paved with the skulls of ambitious priests." (in *De Sacerdotio*) Ambition is like drinking seawater, the more you drink, the more you want.

You will discover the painful truth that some people will undermine your influence when your leadership is announced. Some of these people will be very close to you. Do not lose heart.

There is a flip side to this negative aspect of leadership.

II. Your best support may come from the most unlikely places.

The two characters Pumbaa the Warthog and Timon the Meerkat, the unlikely heroes who rescued Simba from the Vultures, turned out to be his best friends. They accepted him as he was, not for what he could do for them. Even when he revealed his future leadership, Pumbaa and Timon remained loyal and faithful friends. How many of us have experienced the disappointment of instrumental friendship. When we were no longer useful to someone, the friendship and the phone calls stopped. Pumbaa and Timon were faithful to the end and they were rewarded for their steadfastness. There will be people who stick with us, through thick and thin. There will be others who drop by the wayside. Some of those will not be the people we would have predicted.

When Jesus chose his disciples, they were not the "cream of the crop" of Jerusalem society. They were not on the Social Register. They were ordinary folk, fishermen, tax-collectors, people of the land. Who would have chosen Peter to be the leader of the Church? Weak and vacillating in his personal life, he wouldn't have registered very high on the Performax scale. The Apostle Paul wouldn't have even passed the MMPI. Yet these unlikely leaders turned the world upside down and in a few short generations, the Christian message was sent to the known world.

Remember that your best support may come from unlikely places.

III. When you accept your leadership, don't hold back.

When Simba was reminded who he was by his friend and sweetheart, Nala, he came back and asserted his leadership and rightful claim to the position that Scar had usurped.

Those of us who are fortunate enough to have supportive spouses know how powerful it is to have someone love us in spite of ourselves. In those discouraging moments in ministry which come to us all, like Nala in *The Lion King*, these generous spouses call us back to our rightful selves and remind us who we are and who we can be.

When Simba remembered who he was, he had the strength of ten.

In Tennyson's *Sir Galahad*, he speaks of The Pure Heart:
> My good blade carves the casques of men,
> My tough lance thrusteth sure,
> My strength is as the strength of ten,
> Because my heart is pure.

The "enemy" cannot withstand the onslaught of goodness and righteousness. There is an image in Matthew's Gospel of Jesus giving Peter the keys to the Kingdom, and saying, "The gates of Hell shall not prevail against it." We usually think of this passage as the church being "A Mighty Fortress" fighting off the forces of evil. But the truth of the matter is that goodness and truth are on the offensive, and the gates of Hell are giving way. It would make a lot of difference in our ministry and our society if that were the case.

Jesus, Paul, the Martyrs, Luther, Wesley, Martin Luther King, Jr. did not hold back and *neither should we!* There is no force so strong as the force of an idea whose time has come. The time has come for the leadership to rise up and claim the land. We have supported every Cause but Christ for the last two decades and the result has been disastrous.

In his recent book *Church Leadership*, Lovett Weems quotes Faulkner:

> That which is destroying the church is not the
> outward groping of those within it
> or the inward groping of those without, but
> the professionals who control it and who
> have removed the bells from its steeples.

What a powerful picture of the plight of a church which has no witness to proclaim, no message to share, no bells to ring. We are suffering from a loss of leadership.

Weems says: "We need to put the bells back in the steeples and ring out a clear and sure message of faith and hope. We need to ring out that message until every valley is lifted up and every mountain brought low, until the crooked paths are made straight and all the rough ways are made smooth, until all humanity might come to know the salvation of our God. We need a renewal of passion in ministry. We need a ministry characterized by a passion that can come only from a compelling message and an essential mission."

Let's put the bells back in the steeples and ring out a clear message of hope and commitment to Christ. This is not the time for "the sound of uncertain trumpets."

The movie *The Lion King* reminds us that when your leadership is announced, someone close to you might betray you. Yet your best support may come from the most unlikely places. When you accept your leadership, don't hold back. Someone is counting on you to fulfill your calling.

Jesus asked Peter at Caesarea Philippi, "Who do people say that I am?" Peter answered, "You are the Christ, the Son of the Living God." (vs. 16)

Who do people say that you are? You are leaders called by God for ministry and mission to God's people. Remember who you are!

I close with a poem by Warren Molton which is more of a prayer.

> I could have sold most anything
> But you called me to be a pastor,
> And here I sit among the people:

      Pushing prayers,
      Swapping jokes,
         Trading self-esteem for longevity
         Begging for building funds,
          Rustling a Catholic now and then
          Hawking the urban problems
          Picking pockets with committees and boards
           Pirating among the open pulpits
           Auctioning God to the lowest bidder.
Lord, just exactly what was it you had in mind when
   we talked so long ago?
Would you please go over it just one more time?